LEARN ENGLISH without teachers

An immigrant shares
16 techniques that work

Chez Raginiak

ISBN 10: 0-9825071-1-9
ISBN 13: 978-0-9825071-1-7

Visit Chez's website for versions
of this book in other languages.
www.1moment.us

Published by Chez Raginiak
1Moment, LLC
P.O. Box 5555
Hopkins, MN 55343 USA

chez@1moment.us
(651) 775-4294

Printed in China

I dedicate this book to all generations
of immigrants to America, and to
my mother, whom I had to leave behind
without a word of goodbye.

You don't have to live like a refugee!

~ **Tom Petty**

CONTENTS

INTRODUCTION

A message to my fellow immigrants:

I was born in Poland. A communist regime was destroying the lives of my people when I and thousands of others participated in anti-government strikes during the late 1970s. We were arrested and beaten, and some died. With the arrival of martial law in 1981, many of us lost all hope that life could be different, better, happier. I made a decision to escape my beautiful but oppressed country and look elsewhere for freedom. I left my parents, brothers, sisters, friends, and my homeland—forever. I ended up tired, hungry, scared, and penniless in a refugee camp in Austria. I was homesick as never before.

Most of us today don't come to America by way of a long boat ride across the ocean the way generations of immigrants did in years past. But the distance from our families, friends, and homelands is just as far as it was for those immigrants. And, for many, the journey is just as dangerous and heartbreaking. We make sacrifices, compromises, and difficult decisions on our way to freedom and opportunity. Our reasons for coming to a new country are as numerous and as complex as each one of us—from escaping a death sentence for opposing an oppressive government to finding a better job and a more promising life.

The fact that we have arrived here at all is proof that each of us possesses highly developed survival skills. We left so much behind, and we came to America with little but the hope that we can now create "good" lives for ourselves and our families.

But how does one define a "good" life? For some of us, a good life simply means having basic survival needs—food, shelter, a sense of safety, and a job. Once basic needs are met, we can truly begin to thrive.

Thriving goes a few steps further to include:

- belonging somewhere,
- feeling at home,
- being a part of the community,
- making a difference in the world, and
- the feeling of a life well-lived.

These are the things that bring fulfillment. We, the immigrants to this country, can also add an extra factor: the satisfaction of a "mission accomplished"—that our decision to leave our native country and come to America has given a solid foundation to our lives and for our children and grandchildren.

But, my friends, our success with all of these factors starts with language—the English language.

REALLY? NO TEACHERS?

Let me be clear—nothing can replace formal education. However, for many of us—especially those who come here as parents and must have income right away to support our families—going to school is often a luxury of time and/or money we cannot afford.

I did not take any formal classes when I first arrived in America. At that time, I was not ready or able to cross that bridge. I call it a "bridge" because education is the path that can lift someone from poverty to an enriching life. Education can take a person from the bottom of the socio-economic ladder to the top, just as it has for many immigrants to this country.

After twelve years here, I finally did take some English classes, and a year later I signed up to earn a college degree in computer programming. *Computer programming? I did not even know how to type!* But earning a college degree was without a doubt the best investment I made here. I encourage you to do the same when you can. Any degree. Any education. Anywhere.

But, first…

In order to survive in a new country, buy groceries, pay for gasoline, or obtain my driver's license, *I had to speak and understand the language.* This need was my motivation from the very beginning for finding creative ways to learn how to speak English.

These 16 techniques for learning English are the ones that worked for me, and I know they will enable you to learn *while* you are trying to live your challenging new life and make a new home for yourself and your family.

DO YOU NEED FURTHER MOTIVATION?

During my first month in the U.S., one of my sponsors (from the church that helped me come to America) took me to a basketball game at the local high school. On our way to the game, with his mouth facing my ear, he practically shouted, "There will be lots of people there!"

My friend seemed to think that if he spoke more loudly to me, I'd be more likely to understand him. "Okay" was a word that I knew very well by then, so rather than try to communicate that my hearing was fine, I just replied, "Okay."

During those early years I often had to repeat my requests to waiters and cashiers at grocery stores, gas stations, or restaurants. It was not their fault that they could not understand what I was saying. But whenever that happened, I felt angry, frustrated, and embarrassed. I did not want to feel stupid or like a second-class citizen in "the land of equality."

Many of us are likely to be treated in ways that can make us feel, yes, stupid—even if we are fluent in one or more other languages, or have advanced education from another country. I experienced ongoing misunderstandings that led to frustration and discomfort.

The solution was simple: *learn English!*

SAVE THE CHILDREN.

First-generation immigrants often do not realize the potentially disastrous consequences to our children when we do not learn English well enough to communicate with school officials, friends, and with our children themselves (who learn English more easily and quickly than we do).

Children naturally want to fit in. If we don't make the same effort to fit in to our new environment, our children can become distant and feel ashamed of us in public, or when they are around their friends. If we don't understand English, we don't really know what kind of difficulties or troubles our children might be experiencing. Our teenagers could even be buying or selling drugs in our own homes without us knowing.

Protect your children from falling into a dark and often dangerous world where they are influenced by others instead of by you. Protect them from losing everything you tried to give to them by coming to America in the first place. Learn English and stay in tune with their lives, problems, and pains. As children of immigrants, they have plenty enough to deal with.

GUARANTEE YOUR HERITAGE.

I know how much we each value our individual heritage, and how much we want our children to speak our native language and carry on our religious, cultural, or family traditions. I still pray in Polish with my daughters, and our favorite meal consists of Polish bread with Polish cheese and sausages. But more importantly, I can communicate with them and their friends in English; I can help them with their homework and understand their jokes. I want my daughters to feel proud of me when they are with their friends and peers. I know that by learning English I helped to create trusting relationships with my children and motivated them in important ways.

Behavior is not something that can be forced. Children learn from the behaviors we model. There is no better way for us to model desirable behavior than to show that we can be good learners while also carrying on our other responsibilities. When we are admirable role models, our children will carry on our heritage, our ideals, and our memories—not because we forced them to do so, but because they want to.

Learning English will help you create and preserve your family unity and enable your family to live the kind of life you were hoping for here—a happy and fulfilling one.

GRATITUDE GOES A LONG WAY.

My mother was eleven when World War II began. She heard bombers flying over the city and felt the explosions. Her most vivid memory was of German soldiers breaking into her parents' home and taking away her parents. All five children, ages four through thirteen, were left alone with no money for food or heat. My grandfather was forced into hard labor at Auschwitz—the largest death camp ever built.

The children moved to their uncle's house where they spent the next several years. Michael, the youngest, pushed his nose against the window every night, praying for Mommy to come back. On a cold night in the fall of 1944, he came away from the window and ran outside, screaming, "Mommy is home! Mommy is home!"

Yes, she returned, barely more than skin and bones, hairless, but alive. After almost four long, hungry, heart-broken, homesick, children-missing years as a work-camp prisoner, my grandmother was reunited with her children.

A few days before my grandfather was sent to the gas chamber in 1943, he gave a song he wrote as a final message for my grandmother to another Auschwitz prisoner who survived the war and sang it to her. Here is the last line of his "singing message" from Auschwitz:

The end is near, soon I will die.
It's time, my dear, to say goodbye.

Whenever I am tempted—by some minor inconvenience or complaint—to take for granted the opportunity and privileges I have in the U.S., I pause and remember the hardships my family endured and also those brave people who built this country and sacrificed their lives for the freedom we can now enjoy.

We, as first-generation immigrants to this wonderful country, not only have the chance to utilize the freedoms and material comforts made possible by current citizens and previous generations, we also have an obligation to add our part to the richness of the fabric of this nation to make it better, stronger, and more beautiful than ever.

And it all starts with learning the English language.

Throughout my journey from one country and culture to another, I developed and practiced all of the exercises I present in this book, and now I pass them along to you, my fellow immigrants.

Learn English Without Teachers is my needle-and-thread gift that I want you to use in beautifying and strengthening the fabric of your family and this nation.

And now … 16 techniques that work.

TECHNIQUE #1:

Ask for a little help.

Asking is the beginning of receiving...

~ Jim Rohn

A critical factor in your success will be to identify a person who speaks English as a native language, and who is willing to be available to you. Even if this person is available for only a few minutes a day, he or she can still help you with pronunciation. If possible, ask several people to help you in this way.

From the first day I arrived in America, I asked for help from native English speakers (my future friends in many cases). Family, neighbors, friends, teammates, and even strangers helped me to pronounce a word or build a grammatically correct sentence. Even after many years, I still do this. With access to the Internet, we can now refer to online dictionaries and click on the little speaker 🔉 beside a word and listen to pronunciations. (Do that several times and repeat each time.) Listening to a real person speak is also important.

This method will compel you to talk to people, make friends, and better understand your neighbors, coworkers, and the world around you.

TIPS

1. Take a moment to list a few people who might help you with this.

2. Ask if they are willing to go over some words or sounds as you learn.

3. Ask for person's contact information (such as phone numbers and email addresses) and arrange to have a conversation by phone or in person on a regular basis.

List of people I can contact and their phone numbers, etc.:

1.

2.

3.

4.

5.

TECHNIQUE #2:

Be brave.

We cannot change the hearts of other men by mechanism. But only by changing our own hearts and speaking bravely can we surmount the fear that haunts the world today.

~ **Albert Einstein**

Learning any foreign language is hard without bravery. One of the most difficult things for a foreigner to say in English is this sentence: "I'm sorry; I don't understand what you mean." It has nothing to do with pronouncing the words. Instead, it has to do with embarrassment and the fear that people will make fun of us or insult us for not being able to understand.

I can't remember how many times, during my first few years of living in the United States, I was asked about something and answered, "Yes" (or smiled and nodded my head in agreement), while having no clue what I was asked to do. It was just too difficult and embarrassing to say, "Sorry, I do not understand what you asked."

We need to be brave if we want to learn a new language. Being brave is a huge part of open and honest communication between people at any time—especially between foreigners and native-English speakers.

What I found, and what you will probably discover, is that most people won't laugh at you. In fact, just the opposite will happen—they will respect you more for asking, and they will treat you like an intelligent and honest person. So have the courage to say, "I don't understand," when you don't. Have the courage to say, "Could you repeat that, please?" if you did not get it. Courage and persistence will help you to learn the language quickly and correctly. They will also help you preserve your dignity and your honesty.

It is nobody's fault that we may be difficult to understand at first. Learning a new language is a long process—becoming frustrated or impatient won't help. It's much harder to relearn something than it is to learn it correctly in the first place, so don't let fear keep you from asking for help. Be brave and keep asking until you understand.

Bravery also goes beyond asking others for help. Bravery includes such basic tasks as practicing new words on your own in front of a mirror. "Play" with your throat, mouth, and tongue in order to create a new sound that you have not made before.

I still ask friends how to pronounce a word each time I am not sure. They know I also want to SEE how the sound or word is being pronounced, how the sounds are created, and what position the mouth, teeth, etc., are in. This effort adds up to correct articulation on my part and better communication with everyone.

Have the courage to ask a native-English-speaking person to say the sounds slowly and clearly. I found in my experience that people actually like to "show off" their knowledge of the native language. By asking them, we make them feel good and smart, and they don't mind helping us at all. We just need to have the courage to ask, to say, and to repeat it again and again.

Have the courage to ask for help!

TIPS

1. Write down a few basic responses, such as, "Sorry, I did not understand what you said," "How do you say this in English?" or "Can you say it again slowly, please?" Practice them, so you are ready when you need to use them.

2. Start with your children, your family, and your friends. For fun, say to one of them, "Sorry, I did not understand what you said. Could you repeat that, please?" Watch their reaction. You will see that they will try harder and feel good that you care enough to understand everything they say.

3. Listen to talk shows on radio or television, including interviews and White House conferences. You will see that even the leaders of our country and trained native-English speakers often ask for clarification—there's no shame in that. Learn from them and understand that it is the right thing to do.

4. Practice at work. Whether it is a small group meeting or a gathering for the whole company, do yourself (and often, all those around you) a favor and ask for clarification or for someone to repeat a question or statement that you did not understand. BE BRAVE!

TECHNIQUE #3:

Listen to music.

Where words fail, music speaks.

~ **Hans Christian Andersen**

When I was playing in a rock-and-roll and a polka band in Poland, we learned popular English songs by Led Zeppelin, the Beatles, and others. We learned the words phonetically and had no idea what we were singing. But we thought we sounded like our music idols. It wasn't until I came here and started to sing those songs that I realized what a poor job we had done. After I sang a Rolling Stones song, one guy said, "Your language sounds *almost* like English."

That was a very humbling experience, and it taught me how much work I still needed to do to learn the correct pronunciation of English words. But it didn't change the way I feel about music. Like most people, I love music. I have been singing since I could first walk and talk.

Music is one of the best tools for learning any language. Studies show that music activates and engages numerous parts of the brain and improves communication between the brain's right and left hemispheres. Music may be a powerful tool in different types of learning, including language development.[(1)]

When my oldest daughter was eight, I was determined to teach her my native language. Every day I gave her three new words to memorize. I had her repeat each word three hundred times. When I came home from work, I tested her. She remembered them all—good girl! At the same time, for fun, I played some kids' songs, danced with my child, and helped her with articulation. Guess what? Ten years later, she remembered few of the words she memorized, but she still remembers the songs she heard only a few times.

After arriving in a new land, many of us wish to meet people from our old country, eat favorite foods from our native kitchens, and listen to familiar music. But by listening to songs recorded in the new language, not only will you have good practice with English, you may actually enjoy old hits by the Beach Boys, the Beatles, Elvis, or Tom Petty. Especially songs like, "You don't have to live like a refugee!" Because—you don't!

The power of music is incredible. Stimulate your brain. Listen to music… *in English!*

TIPS

1. Sing along with the songs.

2. Write down individual words you recognize. Practice saying those words again and again.

3. Listen to different types of songs.

4. Buy the music you enjoy the most.

5. Try to translate the words to your favorite songs from your native language into English.

6. Sing them!

---

(1) Dr. Lawrence Parsons, University of Texas-San Antonio.

TECHNIQUE #4:

Read out loud.

Reading is to the mind what exercise is to the body.

~ **Joseph Addison**

Many books were not easily accessible to me in communist Poland, so when I arrived in the U.S., I read books on finance, business, self-improvement—on everything! Reading to myself, I could read quickly. Even though I didn't understand all the words, I was able to understand the meaning. Like many people reading a book that is not written in their native language, I just skipped over words I couldn't pronounce.

One day my daughter Monika, who was ten at the time, asked me to read a book to her. What a rude awakening! I stumbled over many of the words—in a children's book! My daughter had all sorts of fun correcting my pronunciation. I was disturbed to think—what if this had happened in front of people at work during a company meeting instead of at home with one of my children?

I started reading together with each of my daughters. We took turns reading out loud and, let me tell you, my daughters were a demanding audience. I think they enjoyed "picking on Daddy."

Reading out loud, especially in front of other people, forces us to try harder, seek help, and SAY each word as it should be said. It taught me to better articulate words, and it improved my spelling.

There is nothing better than reading to improve language skills. With access to computers and word processing programs, it is easy to look up new words in the thesaurus or online. Within seconds we can choose a new word, learn it, and hear how to pronounce it.

More and more children's electronic products can be useful, such as the Children's Talking Dictionary and Spell Corrector. Interactive speaking dictionaries include definitions of words, phonetics, and other helpful features that can enhance our vocabulary.

TIPS

1. Read OUT LOUD everything you see: names of stores, gas stations, street signs, and billboards.

2. Turn on the "subtitle" option on your television and try to read along with the commentators.

3. Borrow children's books from the library and read them out loud.

4. If you have young children, read to them out loud in English. Have them read to you in English, and repeat what they have said. Read for pronunciation practice, to build vocabulary, and for comprehension.

5. Read your children's homework out loud.

6. Read something out loud to your kids or friends in your native language to feel comfortable and capable while reading out loud.

7. Read about things you are passionate about. Music and business were exciting topics for me to read about at first, but perhaps for you it will be sports, motorcycles, home decorating, or cooking. It's your choice. Have fun!

TECHNIQUE #5:

Listen to "talk" radio.

I'd sit alone and watch your light
My only friend through teenage night
And everything I had to know
I heard it on my radio.

~ **Freddy Mercury, "Radio Ga Ga"**

Most newcomers to this country, depending on age, say they enjoy the variety of radio stations and music available in America. I used to listen to *Cities 97* and *KQRS* when I first arrived in Minneapolis. Soon, however, the quantity and quality of commercials got on my nerves. I started noticing that the ends of songs were cut in order to squeeze in more commercials. That was my introduction to commercial radio and the commercial world.

With tape players, then CD players, iPods, satellite radios, and now "who-knows-what" players, we can listen to anything we want in our cars and homes—anytime, anywhere. But constant listening to music (and commercials) can go only so far in one's life. That's how I discovered "talk radio."

Soon, I realized what a great English lesson I was receiving. Thanks to "talk radio," I was learning how to recognize different accents and nationalities, how popular the English language was around the world, and how learning it better would allow me to communicate in just about any country. With time, I became a loyal listener to talk-radio stations. I still am. Not only do I get the news, the weather, great stories, and some music, but, most of all, I listen to English—the language that we, as foreigners, are always learning. Listening to the radio is a convenient and FREE lesson—a lesson of pronunciation, accents, culture, politics, and life in general in our new nation.

When my English was good enough to sound out the words I heard on the radio, I took my "listening" to the next level—I started to repeat all I could after the radio announcers or their guests. I have the most fun trying to sound like speakers from England or Australia—what a challenge!

Knowing English can help you anywhere in the world. In 1991, I visited my cousin in Germany. He had just moved there from Poland, so his German was still at a very basic level. One day he and I went shopping for baby formula, while his wife and a hungry baby waited at home. We walked into a small store, and my cousin asked the salesperson there to help us. The conversation went quite poorly, and he gave up after hearing, "Ich verstehe nicht" (I don't understand), from her several times.

Finally, I gathered enough courage to approach the lady myself. I said in English, "Excuse me. Can you help me find the baby formula?" To my great surprise—and especially my cousin's—she said, "Sure. Follow me."

Listen to talk radio, even if it is playing commercials about baby food. Turn driving time—or working on your yard, car, or any house project—into an English lesson. Switch your dial to talk radio and… listen, learn, repeat!

TIPS

1. Find several talk-radio stations in your area. Listen to each for a while and decide what meets your taste and style. Find out what programs are available and when, so you can tune in to those you like.

2. Listen and try to mimic how the words are pronounced.

3. Tell the stories you hear to your children, family, friends, and coworkers. That will not only allow you to practice the words, names, and (perhaps) jokes, it will also bring you closer to the world you live in and allow you to share the information with the people who live and work with you.

TECHNIQUE #6:

Practice difficult words and sounds.

Practice is the best of all instructors.

~ **Publilius Syrus**

Many Americans are surprised to find out that the number "three" (3) is one of the most difficult words for many foreigners to say in English because it combines two foreign sounds that come one after another: the "th" sound and the "er" sound. To say "three" without a great deal of practice is like trying to rub your stomach with one hand and tap your head with the other. At first it is very difficult, if not impossible.

Many other English words and sounds present a great challenge to foreigners. For people from some Asian nations it is hard to pronounce "s" and "l." For Eastern Europeans, "ing" is not easy to say. These are just a few examples.

No matter what sound is difficult for you, the only way to learn it is to practice it. But first, make sure that you learn how to say it correctly. Have a native-English speaker (one of the people you picked in Technique #1) say it several times to you, and be sure to watch, as well as listen, so you can see how the mouth shapes the word or sound.

My first exposure to the "th" sound came while watching old Western movies when I was still in Poland. There was no sound like that in my language, and I had no idea how to make it. Many Poles, and some others, pronounce "th" as "d" in words such as "northern," or as a hard "t" in expressions such as "thank you" (tank you).

I finally learned how to make the "th" sound from one of my sponsors from the small church in Clarion, Iowa, when I first came to America. He articulated the sound so well that we had to wash the windows in his car—on the inside—after he said it a few times. But I learned to say "th" correctly, thanks to him.

The deep, American-like "er," on the other hand, took more work. One Saturday, I started to practice this sound in the morning and told myself that I would not give up until I got it. I rocked in a rocking chair for five hours, "searching" for the sound. Finally, I called one of my sponsors, who was an English teacher, and asked her to make the sound for me. She did, and she "coached" me on how to say it properly. It took another four hours of practice, but finally, I GOT IT!

This still wasn't enough to say "three" correctly, but I think you get the point. You can probably guess that I continued practicing until I finally was able to say the word, "THREE." What a proud moment that was for me.

Even after more than twenty years in America, I continue working to improve my English. I go to "English" classes when I can, and I recently started using a set of accent-reduction CDs. I listen to them and practice in the car while driving. Every time I do something like this to help improve my pronunciation, I see fewer "I have no idea what he just said" looks on people's faces.

The best thing of all about practicing difficult words and sounds is that we can practice them every time we open our mouths.

Practice difficult words over and over… *in English!*

TIPS

1. When having a difficult time pronouncing a new sound, ask the native-English-speaking person (from your list) to say it to you again and again, very slowly and clearly. Listen carefully. Watch his/her mouth, tongue, teeth. Try to say it. Do it until you get it.

2. Record that sound several times. Leave three seconds between each sample, so you have time to repeat it.

3. Practice what you have learned. Incorporate the newly learned sounds into your vocabulary. For fun, try to use

words that include the new sound. Talk to native-English speakers and see if they are better able to understand what you are saying.

TECHNIQUE #7:

Repeat to remember.

I hear and I forget. I see and I remember.
I do and I understand.

~ **Confucius**

I memorized more difficult words during my first year in America.

While studying German in Poland to prepare for my "great escape" to Austria, I was told by a linguist that if a new word in a foreign language is repeated three hundred times, it should be permanently registered in our memory.

Repeating the same word over and over can become boring quickly. Though this didn't seem like a very creative way of learning a new language, it sounded like an exercise I could do while walking, driving, or even watching television. So I tried it. The interesting thing about the "repeat to remember" approach is that even after repeating a difficult word several hundred times, I found myself forgetting it the next day. However, sometime later, I was nicely surprised to find that I *did* actually remember it.

My first job in America was very monotonous and did not require much brain usage. A printing press put sections of a paper together, stapled them and, finally, cut the paper to a required size while making a sharp sound, "chop," every two or three seconds. Attracted to the rhythmic sounds of the cutting press, I took ten difficult words to work every day and repeated each word one thousand times to the rhythm of the press. It was fun and effective. I memorized more than two thousand new words in less than one year. The press went, "Chop! Chop! Chop!" I went, "Destiny! Destiny! Destiny!" one thousand times. The press went, "Chop! Chop! Chop!" I went, "Vacation! Vacation! Vacation… *please!*"

Look at the illustration on the preceding page. Do you know what the woman is holding? It's a hand tally counter. Buy that or a pedometer to take it with you on a walk, along with a list of ten new words, and walk, talk, click, walk, talk, click.

The clicker will give "instant gratification." Within a few minutes you can memorize one word. Think about it … in one hour of this type of simple activity, you can memorize at least five to ten new (more difficult) words. If you do that every day, after only one year your vocabulary will increase by 1500 to 3000 new words.

Do it! It's easy!

TIPS

1. While riding on a bus or driving in a car, repeat each word in your mind or out loud for a few blocks or a few miles.

2. To break the monotony of repeating the same word again and again, say the word in your native language every fifth or so time, so you can associate it with the word you are learning. You can envision an action or a subject that the word represents. The memorization will be even more effective if your imagination and other senses are involved in the process.

3. Always, always, always make sure that you know how to correctly pronounce the word you are memorizing. Remember: it is much harder to relearn something than to learn it correctly in the first place. Ask any native-English speaker to SAY the word to you. Write it phonetically if that helps you, or record it. Only then, start memorizing it.

4. Come back each day to the words you memorized the day before. The saying, "Use it or lose it," is true. Incor-

porate the words you have learned into your everyday language. Only then will they stay with you.

Repeat each difficult word at least three hundred times… *in English!*

TECHNIQUE #8:

Think in English.

Language is not only the vehicle of thought;
it is a great and efficient instrument in thinking.
~ **Humphry Davy**

I used to work with a very smart lady from China. She had a great memory and was a good listener. At least I thought so because she always took a second or two before she answered my question or commented about what I had said. When I told her how I admired her for being such a great listener, she said, "No, no, no! It is not what you think, Chez. It takes me a while to answer because I need to translate what you said to Chinese, process it, come up with an answer in Chinese, and finally translate it back to English."

Wow! Did I used to do that?

I did, in the very beginning. But soon I was able to "talk in my mind" using English. This was a natural transition that I didn't notice at first, but it will happen to you, too.

To get better at it, I created imaginary situations or conversations and practiced both sides of the exchange. For example, while still in Austria, I promised myself that I would send my mother the very first few dollars (shillings, actually) that I saved, but with the second few dollars I'd buy myself a guitar. When I was close to having enough money to buy my guitar, I pictured and practiced the conversation I expected to have in German with the music store clerk. I imagined myself walking into the store and saying, "Guten Tag!" then asking to try several guitars, and finally paying for one and leaving the store. I basically created a scene with pretend actors in each role.

When the day arrived, I walked into the store, and it was as if I were reliving it. I may not have been the easiest customer for them to understand that day, but I greeted everybody in the store, selected and purchased a guitar, and left the store with a loud "Auf Wiedersehen," a big smile on my face, and a guitar in my hand. Practicing German in my mind worked like magic.

Other exercises in German included becoming lost and asking for directions, buying tickets to shows, ordering food in restaurants, and many more everyday situations.

Not knowing all the words should not stop you from "thinking in English"—or any language you are trying to learn. Say, "Sorry, I don't know how to say this in English." Most of the time people will figure out what you are trying to say.

This may not be easy when you are first starting to learn a new language, but when you can speak English more fluently, don't waste your energy and "processing power" on translating something twice. As soon as you can SAY something in English, you can THINK it… *in English*—you are in charge of your mind!

TIPS

1. Imagine a simple situation, create "actors" as participants in the situation, and make them talk to each other.

2. Resist the temptation to translate what you hear into your native language. Take the words in for what they are and trust that your mind will understand them. When someone speaks to you, try to answer right away. Avoid a double (or even single) translation.

3. Plan ahead. When grocery shopping, for example, make a list of things you plan to buy (it's helpful to do that, anyway) and imagine going to the store and asking for those products. If you want to buy some bottled water, "practice" finding somebody who works at the store and asking where you can find bottled water, and how much it costs. Imagine several different answers you might be given, and practice responding to all of them. Remember to practice "Thank you" at the end.

Make it easy on yourself and think... *in English!*

TECHNIQUE #9:

Create in English.

All children are artists. The problem is how to remain an artist once he grows up.

~ **Pablo Picasso**

On my sixteenth Christmas I received the best present ever from "Santa"—an acoustic guitar. I found it under the Christmas tree… where I put it the night before. My parents could not afford such an expensive present, so I saved enough money during the summer and bought the gift for myself. Until now, the whole family wondered who bought that guitar for me.

There were neither music teachers in town nor music stores, so my only source of music was a radio and one of our neighbors—an amateur guitar player. Slowly but surely I learned the old tunes by the Animals ("The House of the Rising Sun," of course), the Beatles ("Yesterday" and "Let It Be," to start with), and some by Jimi Hendrix. By the summer of 1977 I knew about one hundred guitar chords, and I began writing my own songs. During that summer I wrote one song per day. None made the American or Polish "Top 40," but many of them became my hometown's hits for years to come.

At that time in my life, I did not let my limited talent or my lack of musical training and professional supervision stop me from writing songs. I did not care what others were going to say about the fruits of my creativity. I simply enjoyed the beauty and the freedom of creating something out of nothing, something that was totally MINE, that came from my heart, and that told a story I lived through or witnessed.

Later, in America, I switched from a guitar and writing songs to a computer and writing stories and poetry. When I started dating, I wrote love notes in English. It was difficult to do with the limited English I knew at the time, but it forced me to look up words in the dictionary and pay attention to sentence structure and punctuation. It most definitely expanded my vocabulary.

Writing this book has been another stretch for me. I did research about language and how people learn. I expanded my view on many aspects of life but, most of all, I practiced my creativity, and I did it … in ENGLISH!

If you have a talent or desire to write poetry, stories, books, songs, or speeches—do it. And do it in English. Nothing will motivate you more to improve your new language than creating and perfecting your own "masterpiece," even if nobody else ever sees or reads it. Start with simple, short words. Remember: some of the most powerful stories, titles, proverbs, wisdoms, and quotes used simple one- or two-syllable words. Consider President John F. Kennedy's famous remark: "Ask not what your country can do for you; ask what you can do for your country." These words are almost all single syllables. Isn't that impressive? Or listen to the chorus of "Let It Be." Only a few words are more than one syllable. That is why the song is so easy to learn and sing after only one listening. Learn from the best—let your mind do the rest.

Let your creative juices flow… *in English!*

TIPS

1. If you have school-age children, follow their homework and write an essay each time they have to write one. Read it to your kids. Have fun with it. Kids will love you for it even if your essay is (in their opinion) not very good.

2. Surprise your spouse, children, family, or friends with a poem or a "Thank You" note. Try to be creative while writing. Stretch your imagination. Find and use new words. Deliver them with pride—you should be proud of yourself.

3. Write a daily diary. Any writing is good. Whenever we write, we actually practice the words three times: we say them (or think them), we write them, and we read them. It's a wonderful opportunity to let your imagination fly.

4. Write new words to one of your favorite songs. Or listen to music with no lyrics and write your own.

5. Write down the story of when and how you came to America. Not only will you practice writing and be creative, you will be preserving a memory and creating a treasured story for future generations.

6. Join a writers group. With or without talent, if you keep on writing, you and your family will soon benefit a great deal.

TECHNIQUE #10:

Learn popular sports and play them.

You can observe a lot just by watching.

~ **Yogi Berra**

If you find a sport that you like and a team you would root for (and there are plenty in every city), you will learn the new language much faster by watching or playing the game. At that point, learning a new language (the language of the sport) is not a chore anymore; it is fun! It is your show of appreciation.

I watched my first soccer World Cup here in America in 1986, when it was hosted by Mexico. I watched it with my Polish roommate, and I think we were the only two soccer fans in the whole town even though the World Cup is the largest sporting event in the world. But that's okay. I knew that soccer was not the "American Sport" yet.

The following year I moved to Minneapolis, Minnesota—the land of 10,000 lakes. Besides hundreds of lakes in the Twin Cities, I found thousands of banners advertising the Minnesota Twins baseball team. Baseball was a totally unknown sport to me, a guy from Eastern Europe. Although the Twins won the World Series that fall, I had childishly decided I was going to "pay" America back for its collective disinterest in soccer in 1986 by ignoring baseball. But it did not work out that way.

During the early fall of that year I joined a rock-and-roll band and played bass guitar. We met several times a week at our drummer's house in the heart of Minneapolis. During our first practices, instead of going downstairs, everybody (except me) was glued to the television each time the Twins played. My "Let's go, guys!" had little effect on them. Actually it had a negative effect—we were all becoming frustrated with each other. They wanted to watch something I did not care about, and I wanted to practice. One night I gave up and asked them to explain the rules to me. They did. As a result, one hour later I was spellbound by the TV just as they were. We had fun. A lot of fun! Then we went downstairs and had a great practice.

By learning the rules of baseball, I achieved the following:

- I created and improved the camaraderie between me and my band members.

- I learned many words that helped me in understanding and enjoying the game and also in everyday conversation. Many people use expressions that we, as foreigners, don't understand because they are metaphors borrowed from sports, such as, "throw a curve ball," "home run," or "cover all the bases."

- I was taught an important culture lesson and learned about a part of American history that goes back more than one hundred years, and a game that created many sports heroes and role models.

- I gained even greater appreciation for baseball when one day I tried to hit a ball that was thrown at me by a machine at seventy miles per hour. I did not even see that ball! And those hitters can hit a ball that often travels at a speed of more than ninety miles per hour!

Learn the rules of popular sports. Watch and enjoy. Trust me; they are as good as soccer, cricket, or your favorite sport. Knowing and cheering for a local team, or any team, will give you some fun and something to talk about with neighbors and coworkers.

TIPS

1. Pick a new sport that you may not be familiar with. Find someone who can explain to you the rules, insights, and strategies. Watch some games with that person and make sure that you understand the rules.

2. Pick a team that you like in this sport. You may learn that men or women from your old country play here. The NHL has many hockey players from Eastern Europe, and many baseball players are from Central America. Perhaps having players from your homeland will make you become a fan of that team. If you have a favorite team, you will more fully enjoy the drama, passion, and fun of the sport.

3. Teach the sport and the rules to your children and/or friends. Play it. Use the language to communicate during the game.

Sports are fun. Learn the rules, watch, and cheer… *in English!*

TECHNIQUE #11:

Develop a hobby; find a passion.

Today is life—the only life you are sure of. Make the most of today. Get interested in something. Shake yourself awake. Develop a hobby. Let the winds of enthusiasm sweep through you. Live today with gusto.

~ **Dale Carnegie**

One of my coworkers was not very talkative. I contacted him by email several times, nagging him about assignments that we were both responsible for. The longest answer I ever got from him was, "Great idea!" But one day an email arrived from him that was a page long. I assumed that he was finally addressing all my questions and messages. But as I started reading Steve's email, I saw that it was all about a homeless kitten that was found in front of our building. His email was full of love and concern, details and suggestions. You see, Steve loves cats. He has two of them, knows all about them, and takes excellent care of them. They are like his children. He reads about them and studies them. Cats are his passion.

Steve opened his heart and let the words fly from his fingertips as he typed the email seeking a home for the kitten. That is exactly how we behave with something we love.

I did that with music and playing in the band. I could hardly speak English, but I was learning lyrics, names of songs, bands, music stores, books, guitars, and amplifiers. Within a year I could have talked to Phil Collins about drum sets or to Eddie Van Halen about guitars. (Too bad I never had the chance.)

Finding a special interest, especially if it is a continuation of a hobby we enjoyed in our native country, is like being reunited with a best friend or with a food we liked so much when we were little. Doing what we love helps us survive the most difficult days or years in a new country. Whether it is fishing or mushroom picking, pottery or stamp collecting, cooking, photography, or cats—it doesn't matter. Whatever it is, use it to learn English, increase your vocabulary, and meet people.

Pursuing a hobby is a big step to a better life in a new place. Take that step.

TIPS

1. If you had hobbies you have ignored, get back to them. Start looking in books, online, or at the library for fellow hobbyists in your area. Contact them.

2. Start pursuing what you love. Become an expert in the area, and your vocabulary will grow.

3. If you did not have a particular hobby before, take some time to discover what you are passionate about.

TECHNIQUE #12:

Become active in the community.

Communication leads to community, that is,
to understanding, intimacy, and mutual valuing.

~ **Rollo May**

A month after I arrived in America, I joined the band at my new church. I wanted to get involved in my community right away, but I couldn't sing in English yet, so I played guitar.

I didn't jump into everything that quickly. It took twenty years for me to volunteer to coach my daughter's soccer team. They won the season!

It doesn't have to take *you* twenty years to realize that your church needs help, or that your child's school needs volunteers for a fundraiser or chaperones for a school trip. All these roles are important and, unlike in many other countries with different political systems, many American institutions depend on volunteers in order to be successful and effective.

You may be tempted to wait until your English is better before becoming active in any organizations. But getting involved *will* help your English and also help you feel more at home in America.

Anna, who came here with her family from Mexico City, joined my Toastmasters Club and volunteered to be the club's treasurer. When it was time to collect dues, she sent a reminder to everybody but did not get too many responses or payments. I suggested she become more "aggressive," sending out more emails and visiting people in person. Right away, new and creative emails started arriving in our mailboxes. Anna used cartoons and stories to keep the requests for money on the light side. That alone forced her to work hard on her language skills. Her English improved every day. Becoming active in the club turned out to be an excellent ego booster for her, an opportunity to practice English, and a great bridge between her and all the members of our club.

As soon as we settle into our new home in America, we should take the very next step on our journey to become fully involved and productive citizens by taking an active role in our communities, places of worship, schools, or even in local politics—just look what Arnold Schwarzenegger did.

We cannot be just observers, evaluators, and beneficiaries of what our new nation offers. It is our home now, after all, and it is important that we become active in the world we live in. This is also an opportunity to improve our English by speaking outside of our homes, with people other than our family and closest friends. You will reap wonderful rewards from volunteering. There is no better feeling in the world than the satisfaction of doing something good without expecting a financial reward.

Become active in the community, schools, churches, synagogues, mosques, and your children's lives. This will not only give you many opportunities to practice English but will also help you make new friends, feel connected, and perhaps find a job. It can make you feel for the first time that "crossing over" to the mainstream culture has meaningful benefits.

Be part of the community and the world around you!

TIPS

1. If you have children in school, find out what volunteer activities are available. Schools rely heavily on parent volunteers and will love you for helping out.

2. Read the "Community Calendar" section of your newspaper. Find a club or organization that interests you. Attend at least one meeting.

3. What hobbies and activities do you enjoy? Find a way to help others using those skills, such as knitting baby caps or blankets for a hospital or relief organization.

4. Attend a city council or school board meeting. Find out about local politics and what's going on in your community.

5. Take a community education class in something that you'd like to learn about, or that you think would be fun, such as computers, cooking, or dancing.

TECHNIQUE #13:

Remain a good student.

For learning to take place with any
kind of efficiency students must be motivated.
To be motivated, they must become interested.
And they become interested when they are
actively working on projects which they can
relate to their values and goals in life.

~ **Gus Tuberville**

A good friend of mine came to the United States with her husband in 1980, so he could finish his doctorate. Their plan was to return to Poland as soon as possible after that, where she had a great job, and they both had family and friends. But on December 13, 1981, martial law was declared in Poland, and it was too dangerous for them to return—many people were being arrested and even killed. So my friend decided to stay in America a bit longer, and then a bit longer. Her husband found a job. They had a child and made a new home for themselves here. But because she always wanted to go back to Poland, she wasn't motivated to learn about America.

I, on the other hand, wanted to live in America for as long as I can remember. I was very interested in all aspects of this nation, and I could not wait to come here. Such desire helped me to arrive with a hunger for learning. I wanted to be a good student.

Being a good student is about choice, and about motivation. I *chose* to learn as soon as I arrived in the United States. Surrounded by a new language, new culture, and with no useful profession, I was motivated from the very start to learn it all. This helped me in every aspect of assimilation, from enthusiastically signing up for English classes and studying this language, to learning about those "strange" sports and even playing them.

Oh, yes, I always knew that even America was far from being a perfect nation, but I could quickly put things in perspective to reignite my love and passion for learning how to live here as fruitfully as possible.

With time, learning, and experiencing new things, my interest in this nation deepened further. I became the type of person who takes John F. Kennedy's question (about what we can do for our country) seriously. I transformed from being a taker to being a giver. From being the one who looks from the outside in, I became one who desires to be on the inside. This book is one attempt to give back—as a citizen of this country with all its privileges and also with the responsibilities that living here requires.

I truly care about this nation and want to do all I can to make our country better. As a result, I am more interested in it than ever. This makes me a good student—even after all these years.

Be a good student and have fun with that!

TIPS

1. Talk to immigrants who left their countries to escape danger. The harsher their experience was, the more they probably appreciate what they have here and now. See how they live, and learn from them. Appreciate life.

2. Talk to immigrants who came here for economic reasons. See if there is a difference in their attitudes to life in America. Compare the two and decide how you feel about it. Pick a road that leads to your happiness.

3. Don't push away what is new or unknown to you. Learn first before you make up your mind. Even if you already have a favorite sport—or food, or music, or type of clothing—be willing to try new ones. You may find a new favorite. But even if you don't, you will experience what becoming a student of life is all about.

TECHNIQUE #14:

Have some fun and don't take little misunderstandings too seriously.

Laughter is the same in any culture.

~ **Dan Brannan**

When his cousins came here from the Ukraine one summer, Dmitry lent them a car and sent them off to see the Black Hills in South Dakota, where they stayed with his American friend. At one point, the friend asked the brothers if they took turns driving when they traveled the country. Looking puzzled, one brother answered, "Of course we took turns! When the road turned left, we turned left. When the road turned right, we turned right!"

They were all rolling on the floor in laughter after Dmitry's American friend explained to them what "taking turns" means in the U.S.

Little misunderstandings like this are common, and there is no need to become upset or embarrassed by them. The English language is filled with slang, idioms, colloquial expressions, and other informal phrases that can be confusing to those unfamiliar with them. Americans laugh easily. They are quick to laugh at themselves and at others. Remember that in most cases they are not being mean or insensitive. People laugh when they hear something funny, but also when they hear something unexpected or surprising. And they are usually surprised when they realize that something they say all the time and take for granted has quite a different meaning to the person hearing it.

This is an excellent opportunity for you to improve your knowledge and understanding of English, and it can help you improve your sense of humor, as well. When someone laughs, and you don't understand why, ask. Do it with a smile rather than a scowl, and they'll usually be happy to explain why they were laughing or whatever it was they found so funny. When you understand the reason for the laughter, you can join in it, too. That may give *you* a funny story to tell others.

Laughter is contagious and good for you. It reduces stress, strengthens the immune system, speeds healing, and helps to connect with others.[(1)] So have fun and don't take little misunderstandings too seriously. Learn to laugh as the Ukrainian brothers did. You'll not only be happier but healthier, too.

Laugh, and the world laughs with you!

TIPS

1. Try not to become frustrated or embarrassed over little misunderstandings.

2. Learn to laugh at these misunderstandings, and at yourself.

3. Ask others what they're laughing about if you don't understand.

4. Do it with a smile.

5. Look for the humor in your everyday life—especially in the things you find difficult.

6. Share funny stories and experiences with others.

---

(1) "The Stress Management and Health Benefits of Laughter," Elizabeth Scott, M.S.; *Your Guide to Stress Management.*

TECHNIQUE #15:

Attitude is everything; be positive.

One of the greatest powers in the universe is individual power of choice. And the most powerful choices are positive choices.

~ **Frederick Mann**

In his book, *Learned Optimism*, Martin Seligman demonstrates that an optimistic outlook on life can be learned. For example, with logic and evidence we can contradict our negative beliefs. We can weaken them and with time (and other methods) bring more positive thinking to our minds. And just as optimism can be learned, so can a strong and positive attitude.

I've tried to teach my kids how to become optimists because I believe optimism is one pillar that supports a happy and fulfilling life.

During the summer of 2007, I received a phone call from the Minnesota Office of Revenue. Yes, one of the worst phone calls a business owner can receive—my company was randomly picked to go through a "sales and use tax" audit, covering the previous three years. No mistakes in our tax filing were found—it was just a routine audit to assure that we were paying what we owed. "No more, no less," as the letter stated. The problem was not in the audit, but in how I started to feel about it. Even after I double-checked all our paperwork and records to ensure that we complied with all requirements, I caught myself feeling nervous, irritated, disappointed, and sorry for myself.

"Why our company out of hundreds of others?" I lamented.

My mood and attitude became so poor that with only one week to go before the meeting, I could not concentrate, my heart felt like it was going to explode, and I had absolutely no energy.

It was time for me to apply what I had learned from Dr. Seligman.

One of his suggestions was physical exercise, so I took a walk—a long walk. I also argued with myself in order to dispute the negative and paralyzing thoughts that had taken over my mind. I thought of situations from my past when I was in much more difficult circumstances but managed to get out of them with no harm done—only lessons learned. For example, I remembered my year in a refugee camp, my grandfather's death in Auschwitz, Grandma's jail time during the war, and my mother with her four siblings surviving the war without their parents. After all that, I realized that my situation wasn't so bad.

"Shape up!" I told myself. "Everything will be all right!"

As a result, I felt better within minutes. My energy returned. I had a big dinner and began looking at the upcoming audit as a necessary evil—not as a depression-initiating disaster. Using exercise, facts, and past experiences helped me improve my attitude about my present life and problems.

Many foreigners have a similar or even more dramatic past, but our current opportunities can be realized only with the right attitude. That applies to everything we do, say, and think—including how we approach learning the new language, culture, and traditions.

With the right attitude we can make our dreams come true, help our families "back home," and do anything our hearts desire.

Learn how to develop, improve, and keep a positive attitude. The success in your life is proportional to your attitude. Build them both.

A good life, no matter where it is, starts with a good attitude.

TIPS

1. When feeling upset, first remove the feeling of catastrophe. Look around your home and life. See that you are in a safe place, that you have food and water, a warm bed, friends, and family. If your life is not in any danger, push away the catastrophic feeling that may have built up in your mind.

2. Use facts to dispute your own thoughts and assumptions. Our mind is often the biggest liar, but we believe it.

3. Try to find the benefits in even the worst of circumstances. If you have lost your job, think about all those times when you wanted to quit it anyway. Look at the situation as an opportunity.

4. Occupy your mind with simple tasks that you can do no matter how you feel. When you have no job, you can work on your resume or collect references. Buy a newspaper and check the employment section. These things can be done easily. Do them.

5. Stay physically fit. The old saying goes, "Healthy body, healthy mind," so put your running shoes on and go for a jog. Using your body will help your mind.

6. When you bounce back and feel great, don't let small things bring you down again. Keep the good attitude. We have only one life—enjoy it!

TECHNIQUE #16:

Strive to be happy.

If you want happiness for an hour, take a nap.
If you want happiness for a day, go fishing.
If you want happiness for a year, inherit a fortune.
If you want happiness for a lifetime, help somebody.
~ Chinese Proverb

Happiness, happiness! We all want it. We all wish for it. In fact, "the pursuit of happiness" is one of the inalienable rights listed in the American *Declaration of Independence.* But happiness means different things to different people. For some it means freedom. For others it is wealth and material possessions. And for many more, it means finding a perfect partner and living happily ever after.

Some confuse happiness with pleasure, but true happiness is more than that. For foreigners, finding happiness in a new, unfamiliar country is challenging. It isn't easy, but it can be done.

Why is it so hard for us to feel happy in a new country? In a study on happiness and how it is affected by our environment, Jennifer L. Koslosky, of the Department of Psychology at Missouri Western State University, identifies strong marriages, family ties, friendships, self-esteem, and spirituality as some of the areas in our lives that contribute to happiness.(1)

For many immigrants, those are exactly the relationships that are torn apart when we leave our homes and loved ones behind, even when it's for a better life. Husbands, wives, siblings, parents, children, and the friends we have known since childhood—many of us had to say goodbye to them all. The hope is always to be reunited someday. Even when we are lucky enough for that to happen, we have often been separated from them for a very long time. When I came to America in 1985, I assumed that my goodbye was forever. For many, it is.

Our self-esteem can be shattered by the time we first arrive in a new country. It's hard to walk with your head held high when you feel constantly confused or simply too lost or scared to carry on a simple conversation.

We are pretty lucky here in America where diverse religions are tolerated. Still, our connections with priests, pastors, rabbis, imams, and other spiritual leaders from our former places of worship are broken. We miss the comfort and familiarity of our churches, synagogues, cathedrals, or mosques back home.

I still miss being able to attend Mass in the beautiful, 700-year-old church from my childhood in Poland. The place filled me with awe and reverence, and provided an atmosphere of unity and spirituality that fed and nurtured my soul from an early age.

What can make things even harder for foreigners is the common belief that regardless of what kind of life we had in our original homeland, we should be happy here—no matter what. Times can be tough wherever we are. In some cases, any slip, mistake, or incorrect behavior on our parts can support and reinforce unfair stereotypes or labels associated with our nationality, or about foreigners in general.

Happiness is a lofty and difficult goal for anyone. But it can be especially hard for foreigners—for those seen as different. That's why it often takes several generations for people to feel at home in America or any new country.

Anyone who is a "foreigner" is acutely aware of how some people do not trust or like those who are different. Despite the temptation to feel alienated, we must try not to dwell on this or assume that everyone is that way. Just be aware that some people may make incorrect assumptions about you based on ignorance or a lack of familiarity.

We, the foreigners, have the same desires and ambitions as anyone. Other than the language and our country of origin, we are similar in the way we dream, have needs and desires, and strive for a full life.

I know that happiness can be found in our new country in one generation. New friendships can be formed. Self-esteem can be rebuilt. Love can be found. Families and marriages can be reunited and strengthened. Faith can be practiced in new surroundings. All this is possible within our lifetime—with the power of our will and mind, the desire of our heart and soul, the work of our feet and hands, and the touch of faith and love.

Follow these tips and travel from learning basic language skills to playing an active role in the lives of your family, neighborhood, community, and beyond, to the most successful life you can imagine, to a happy life in your new home.

TIPS

1. Don't confuse pleasure with happiness. Pleasure is a temporary feeling. Happiness comes from developing strong relationships and self-esteem, and from a sense of accomplishment.

2. Do something extraordinary, good, or helpful, and don't tell anybody about it. Watch your self-esteem grow.

3. Build new friendships. Find new relationships through sports, a good attitude, and involvement in your community. New friends cannot replace your old ones, but friendship is valuable at every stage of your life.

4. Invest in your marriage and in relationships with the people you care about. Don't take love for granted. Cherish it and do all you can to keep the fire going.

5. Incorporate exercises suggested in this book into your daily life. Learn the culture and traditions; learn English with speed and determination. Develop a good sense of humor, enjoy life, feed your mind and heart, and start speaking up for what's right. Reach for the stars, dream, and love yourself and others. BE HAPPY!

---

(1) "Happiness, How our environment affects our well being and performance," Jennifer L. Koslosky, of the Department of Psychology at Missouri Western State University, sponsored by Brian Cronk. http://clearinghouse.missouriwestern.edu/manuscripts/292.asp

FINAL THOUGHTS

Many of the greatest and most well-known Americans were not American by birth, and many of them spoke other languages before learning English. Albert Einstein (born in Germany), wrote in *The World As I See It*: "But without deeper reflection one knows from daily life that one exists for other people—first of all for those upon whose smiles and well-being our own happiness is wholly dependent, and then for the many, unknown to us, to whose destinies we are bound by the ties of sympathy. A hundred times every day I remind myself that my inner and outer life are based on the labors of other men, living and dead, and that I must exert myself in order to give in the same measure as I have received and am still receiving ..."

Not every immigrant will reach the level of accomplishment of Albert Einstein, but we all have the opportunity to excel—to be more and better today than we were yesterday, to pursue freedom and happiness for ourselves and for our children. In America, anything is possible if we desire it, pursue it, and have people who are willing to help us along the way. There is no doubt in my mind that America is full of people who are willing to reach out and help us, but the first move is ours. We need to demonstrate that desire to be active contributors to our communities by doing what every first-generation immigrant must—learn English as quickly as possible.

I know how difficult it is to start a new life in a new country, especially if we have arrived with nothing. Being able to go to school to learn English seems like an unrealistic luxury when we are struggling just to put food on the table and possibly working at two or three low-paying jobs. But something we can do right away is to try to speak English at every opportunity, including at home with the family. It is almost impossible to learn the language if we continue to speak our native language at home. We don't have any other real choice. If we want to feel at home here, we need to learn English. Becoming part of a new country is all about "language, language, language"—especially at first.

America has often been called a melting pot—a place where people of different languages, cultures, and customs come together and enjoy the promise of freedom—to live, work, play, and pray without threats to their individual values and beliefs. When we all work together, we are strengthening the fabric of our community. When we help each other, we help ourselves most of all.

You can do it!

- Ask for a little help.
- Be brave.
- Listen to music.
- Read out loud.
- Listen to "talk" radio.

- Practice difficult words and sounds.
- Repeat to remember.
- Think in English.
- Create in English.
- Learn popular sports and play them.
- Develop a hobby; find a passion.
- Become active in the community.
- Remain a good student.
- Have some fun and don't take little misunderstandings too seriously.
- Attitude is everything; be positive.
- Strive to be happy.

Whoever is happy will make others happy, too.

~ **Mark Twain**

I NEED TO LEARN THE LANGUAGE

I need to learn the language,
So I can tell about my pain,
About my fears,
My desires.
So I can sing with my children,
Guide them,
Pray.

I need to learn the language,
So I can understand the whisper of my destiny,
Follow it,
Fulfill it.

I need to learn the language,
So I can travel the future
With no misunderstood goals,
No mispronounced intentions.

I need to learn the language,
So I can live.

~ Chez Raginiak © 2009
from *MY ESCAPE TO FREEDOM*

PRESENTATIONS BY CHEZ RAGINIAK

FIND HOPE, CHOOSE TO FOLLOW IT, AND GET BUSY.
Refill your heart with hope, energy, and the belief that it is in your power to make the rest of your life the best of your life.

WHAT'S IN YOUR WHEELBARROW?
(Based on an award-winning speech)
Find out how to effectively switch from activities that produce no results to those that provide the greatest rewards.

LEARN ENGLISH WITHOUT TEACHERS.
Learn 16 proven, effective, and fun techniques on how to learn English outside the classroom to assimilate into a culture more quickly.

CREATING THE BEST IMPRESSION.
This fun and interactive session teaches specific techniques to create the best first impression.

For availability and booking
information, contact Chez at:
(651) 775-4294
chez@1moment.us

www.1moment.us

WHAT OTHERS SAY ABOUT CHEZ'S PRESENTATIONS:

Your message is very timely. Everyone needs hope right now and you deliver that message in a very unique and inspiring way.

Frank Sherwood, vice president,
Colliers Turley Martin Tucker

Chez, so many people commented on how great you were. It has been wonderful working with you.

Sandy Gibson, Hennepin County
Human Services and Public Health Department

Thanks for making our meeting (IAAP) great! I really enjoyed your story and humor, and I like your first impression advice—polished look, smile, firm handshake, and rock and roll! ☺ That's great!

Sherry Zupin, executive assistant,
Twin Cities West Chapter, IAAP

You are the greatest! Your enthusiasm and heart will impact many people's lives. You have certainly impacted mine.

Jane Rischmiller,
Rosemount Nuclear Instruments, Inc.

Chez is a gifted professional speaker and author who met the rigorous challenges and dangers embedded in escaping the world of communism and discovering the fruits of freedom. He speaks directly from the heart.

Dr. Lyman K. (Manny) Steil, CSP, CPAE,
author of *Listening Leaders: The Ten Golden Rules to Listen, Lead & Succeed*

We must never be afraid to go too far,
for success lies just beyond.

~ **Marcel Proust**

Notes

Notes

Notes